Windswept

Windswept

S. G. McAfee

ARPress

ILLUMINATING IDEAS.
EMPOWERING VOICES

ARPress
45 Dan Road Suite 5
Canton MA 02021

Hotline: 1(888) 821-0229
Fax: 1(508) 545-7580

Ordering Information:
Quantity sales. Special discounts are available on quantity purchases by corporations, associations, and others. For details, contact the publisher at the address above.

Printed in the United States of America.

ISBN-13:   Softcover   979-8-89389-011-2
                  eBook   979-8-89389-012-9

Library of Congress Control Number: 2019918037

Randi Lyn,

... In all the world God's perfect heart gave
me the gift of you ... My Song

Love you,
Mom

Contents

Introduction

In raging storm
I turn my back against the wind
To gather strength ...
And so it goes
On stormy sea of life
Like biting rain
Grief blows across my aching heart
Relentless
Beating upon my very soul
My breath coming in gasps
Darkness swallows me
Me – lost in deafening silence
Me – bending, unbroken
May compassion touch you
Faith comfort you
And peace enfold you
Adjust your sails
For you cannot change the wind ...

Mr. Blue

He listens when I whistle
He listens when I talk
He listens, listens when I run
And even when I walk

He chirps and chirps – it's really cute
He does it day by day
He chirps as if to tell me
That he's a big Blue Jay!

Although he is not yet full grown
He's actin' pretty smart
For when that big ol' cat walks by
He tears his cage apart

Nature

Nature has so many things
That you and I can see
Birds, trees, butterflies
And even bumble bees!

She also has the moon, the stars
The earth, the sun, the sky
She put them on the list
Along with you and I

My Collie

I have a collie dog
And we have lots of fun
He goes outside to play with me
Until the day is done

He barks and tugs and pulls my hair
It doesn't hurt a bit
For after all it's all in fun
And then at night we quit

Our Savior

Our Savior walked upon the earth
He lived – for us He died
He cleaned our souls from black to white
And with us He abides

Christmas

Christmas is coming
Hooray! Hooray!
Candle light Christmas light
Oh! Are they gay!

A wreath for the door
A prize for the winner
And boy! On the table
There's turkey for dinner

The presents are wrapped
And in all shapes and sizes
Are under the Christmas tree
With laughs and surprises!

My Puppy

My puppy likes to romp and play
And run and bark at me
He does this almost every day
It's really cute to see

He barks at people passing by
And even at the cars
He barks at birds a flying high
And even at the stars

But when he has been very bad
He looks at me above
"I can't whip him," I say to myself,
"It must be puppy love!"

Turkey Strut

You could hear him a squawkin'
As you walked out the door
He thought he owned the place
But he wouldn't much more

"I'm gonna catch 'im," said Pa,
And chop off his head
"And bein's we're tired of chicken
We'll have turkey instead."

He chased him 'round the yard
For an hour at least
But he couldn't catch that turkey
Which he called a feathered beast

As you look into the kitchen
You can see its kind o' late
But the turkey's in the barn
And the chicken's on the plate

Play Ball

Did you ever stop and wonder
How a blade of grass survives?
It doesn't dance, it doesn't sing
It doesn't even sigh

It sits there in the ground and grows
It doesn't move – it's stuck!
But little blade of grass grow tall
The baseball costs a buck!

Greetings

When I'm alone I reminisce
'Bout the good times that we shared
Your class ring that you gave to me
To show me that you cared

Wherever you were, there I was
And vice versa was the same
It seemed when we were spoken of
They echoed just one name

We spoke to mom about our love
She ranted and she raged
But love is blind, our love was strong
And we became engaged

Now Uncle Sam has taken you
I pray that God won't, too
For no greater love will I ever share
With anyone but you

United

Charlie thinks I left here
He thinks I got out fast
He saw demolished villages
He thinks he kicked my ass

He doesn't know that I'm around
That two can play his game
He thinks I have a yellow streak
So now he'll stake his claim

But Charlie let me warn you
While freedom is oppressed
I'll be there always underfoot
I'll never let you rest

Sonny Day

Peeking in the mirror
Falling off the chair
Playing in the toilet
Carrots in his hair

Sitting in the dog food
Talking on the phone
Powdering his wagon
Tasting Pepper's bone

Hiding Daddy's work shoes
Washing Mommy's bed
Cleaning in the trash can
Standing on his head

He's laughter, love and innocence
A bundle full of joy
He's Mommy's little helper
And Daddy's little boy

Best Wishes

From watching my son learn and live
I reminisce and see
A loving, happy childhood
And how much you mean to me

You were always there when needed
You were always so sincere
You would mend my broken dreams and heart
And kiss away my tears

Though I've never really let you know
How much I love you two
I'll tell you now in my own words
I love you, happy anniversary, Sue

A Silent Prayer

Dear God,
    Please listen while I speak
    My heart still breaks, my eyes still weep
    My arms are empty, my mind confused
    His toys, his books, his bed – unused
    I try my best to know he's safe
    To know You have him in Your grace
    But my emptiness and aching heart
    Still sometimes get my better part
    I pray to You to help me now
    To give me strength I lost, somehow
    To give me peace of mind and rest
    To let me know I did my best
    Please kiss and hug him, God, for me
    And when he sits upon Your knee
    For me, would You please smile and say
    That I will hold him on my day

God's View

God made the beauty of the earth
For all of us to view
From the sunrise, sunset, shooting stars
To the mist and morning dew

From the majestic height of mountain
To the humble windy plain
From the wintry snow white blanket
To, in April, soft spring rain

From trees, the grass and flowers
To instincts of the wild
From butterflies and rainbows
To cries of a newborn child

But the best view God has saved for last
In His sacred home above
It's His heaven of eternal life
With the glory of His love

How Much

How I long to see his smile
Hear his voice or feel his touch
How I long to kiss his tears away
Dear God, You know how much

How I long to hear him read to me
Which he never learned to do
How I long to feel his hug while whispering,
"Mommy, I love you."

How I long to hear him whistle
Sing a song or say his prayers
How I long to carry and tuck him in
After falling asleep downstairs

Now I'll never see his smile
Hear his voice or feel his touch
But he'll be there always in my heart
Dear God, You know how much

Angel Mine

The sun doesn't shine so bright now
Since my little boy has gone
And sleep doesn't come enfold me
'Til the breaking of the dawn

Raindrops aren't like diamonds now
Fallin' softly from the sky
And my aching heart can't help but break
When my empty arms ask why

Each day is unfulfilling
When my mind skims the last five years
And as I turn my head from his picture
My eyes fight back the tears

But the breezes seem to whisper
Through the trees in the lonely night
"Sh-h-h, don't cry, he's safe now
He is near though he's not in sight."

Justice for All

As I sit and quietly listen
For the sounds that my heart's missin'
A cry is swallowed in my throat and then
As my eyes search for his smile
My empty arms know all the while
That I'll never hold him close to me again

There was no judge or jury
And the sadness of the story
With a thirty dollar fine he went his way
And the little boy left dyin'
By the car that he was drivin'
Sentenced me to live a lonely life each day

Silent tears and unhealed sorrow
Are what fill each new tomorrow
And knowin' that I'll never watch him grow
Untold pain in my heart hidden
Is a sentence I was given
As the mother of that child
I love him so

Hold Me

My life is not worth it
No matter the pain
The questions – no answers
A face with no name

A yearning a longing
A place to belong
A cold empty feeling
A thought that's all wrong

A bending, a yielding
A comforting touch
A weight on my shoulders
Dear God, it's too much
My life is not worth it
No matter the cost
Everything that I love
Everyone that I lost

One, Two

I have two hands with fingers and thumbs
I have two feet with toes
I have one chin, two ears, two eyes,
And a mouth right under my nose

So Big

When I was small I used my knees
To crawl and climb the stairs
But now I'm big I use my knees
To kneel and say my prayers

At The Edge

What right have I to think that he
Would ever care for lousy me
With two miscarriages and one dead child
Compared to mine his life was mild

It's not that I want sympathy
Or in comparison the better is me
But I've given only half a heart
And in fifteen months it's torn apart

I've never sought out my revenge
On people I consider friends
I say it plural knowingly
If added now there's one plus me

So I'll tell you now or have you heard
That Sue and Frank are separate words
But I've learned to smile up to the end
I pray to God I've still one friend

Shadow of Your Smile

Within the shadow of your smile
Life's glare cannot begin
To scorch our trust and happiness
To make our love a sin

Life tries by using others
That we hold close and dear
Life makes the shadow smaller
It fills our eyes with tears

Our emotions start to smolder
Our shadow starts to fade
The silence makes it kindle
Each moves to find the shade

But together we move closer
And in a little while
Once more our love's protected
In the shadow of your smile

Peninsula

Lie down beside me, darling
Caress me with your eyes
Touch me gently with your whispers
Kiss me softly with your sighs

Lie close beside me, darling
Feel the pent up splendor surge
As we speak with words unspoken
Let the love we have emerge

While the trees seclude our passion
From the peeking stars above
Let your arms partake the splendor
Enfold me in your love

Thanx

When troubles seem to find us
And we know not where to turn
Loving friends and family members
Become filled with deep concern

All life's worries and frustrations
Lessen when we share
You brought comfort and assurance
Just by being there

Wishes

I have no gift or money
On this Father's Day today
I only have a kiss and hug
And something else to say

You've given me so much in life
There's more that I can learn
You both were there to lend a hand
You asked nothing in return

With loving guidance both of you
Have taught me right from wrong
With patient understanding
Both of you have made me strong

I wish you joy and happiness
For all the world to see
Because I love you, Mom and Dad
You mean the world to me

Sharing

It's nice to have dear friends
That you can talk with on the phone
Who'll listen to your worries
When you feel so all alone

Friends who think that you're okay
When you aren't always right
And when at times you feel mixed up
They'll help you see the light

I guess I'll never have much wealth
As far as money goes
But I'm a wealthy person
'Cause, dear friend, you share my woes

One Christmas

He sits there and watches the little toy train
And a small boy sits by his side
He's a fine little lad and he looks like his dad
You can see that his dad's full of pride

His dad lets him blow the train whistle, too
Then they sit there and laugh with delight
He wants daddy to make the cattle car run
If he's good, well, his daddy just might

They could sit there for hours but the night's comin' on
And the little one must go to bed
He will dream of today – of his daddy and train
And tomorrow that lies just ahead

Soon the years will pass by and the lad will grow up
But I'll always remember the sight
Of the boy and his dad with the little toy train
Together and happy that night

Nani

Pop-Pop says you're safe and sound
Living with God above
And all I have to do is say
A prayer to send my love

So Nani here's my prayer
It's sent with hugs and kisses, too
Now I lay me down to sleep
And I'm still missin' you

Gentle Friend

You placed your paw upon my lap
And nudged my hand to stroke your back
With sloppy kisses and waggin' end
You became my Gentle Friend

Down life's path we walked together
"Neath sunny skies and stormy weather
Unknown to us around the bend
Death waited for my Gentle Friend

I trudge life's path with steps unsure
But when I knock on heaven's door
I know the time will come again
When I'll walk with my Gentle friend

Sea Breeze

Sailing on the sea of life
You paused along the way
Touching many lives with kindness
Bringing many brighter days

That's why you're wished the very best
In everything you do
With calm seas and gentle winds
From all of us to you

Always

Bow and say a prayer to God
Telling of your sorrow
That he may comfort and console
To brighten your tomorrow

Through heartache and your darkest hour
Faith will be your guide
Remember you can lean on Him
He's always by your side

Water's Edge

At water's edge I watched my ship
Sail away from me
A journey to another shore
A home across the sea

I waved farewell and sadly watched
My voyager depart
While gentle winds filled empty sails
Tears filled my empty heart

I lingered by the water's edge
Filled with great dismay
I watched my ship sail toward the sun
I had to look away

And on that distant final shore
A joyous song is known
They sing a welcome filled with love
A traveler has come home

Mom

A gentle hug from busy hands
Soothing words that calm
Mix with patience, love and smiles
God creates a mom

Pearl

As constant as the ocean tide
And oyster with its pearl
As long as moonbeams streak the sky
Always daddy's girl

String Bean

Hugs a kiss and laughter
A daughter from the start
Shares secrets, dreams – then with a smile
Shares love and steals your heart

Sonshine

Explore four corners of the earth
Quell the mighty sea
No matter where life leads, son
You mean the world to me

Dad

Gentle hugs that whisper strength
Mix with smiles then add
Whisker kisses, winks of love
God creates a dad

Grandeur

Cherished gifts from heaven
Granddaughters from the start
With a hug and kiss give happiness
Then smile and steal your heart

Grandest

A constant source of pleasure
A grandson from the start
With a hug and a kiss gives happiness
Then smiles and steals your heart

G.H.

Telephone, telegraph, tell AMY! Tell her it's my LUCKY day
The staff at GENERAL HOSPITAL will know I'm on my way
To keep up with the JONES' (A marriage made in heaven)
I'll say hello to LEE and GAIL then pop in and see KEVIN

The air fills with a lullaby approaching MARY MAE'S
I'll help wipe hands and faces, I'll kiss some tears away
If DONELY ever hauled me in to ask me, "What's the word?"
I'd call for JUSTUS by my side then tell him what I heard

"FELICIA'S heart's in FRISCO, SEAN, SAMONE'S heart's broke in two
ROBIN'S got a heart of STONE, what's a 'goil to do?
Nuts to MAC and DAMIEN and MIKE should take a hike
SCULLY leaves me LUKE warm seriously, what is there to like?"

I'll rest upon my LAURELS as SEAN puts my prints on file
He'll notice my new RUBY ring a gorgeous TIFANNY style
I'll visit with dear LILA and while REGINALD pours tea
I'll give thumbs up to let him know his secret's safe with me

I'll chat with EDWARD QUARTERMAINE and ALAN and the BOYS
Then say a prayer for MONICA and toss ANNABELL some toys
I'll swing by the GATEHOUSE and hope to shoot the breeze
With THE IDOL RICH, MIGUEL, LILLY, LOIS and her MAIN squeeze

When I drop in at LUKE'S PLACE I'll tell SONNY and his LADY
Don't cut no slack just watch your back those business deals look shady
A twisted mind that FOSTER'S hate distorts RYAN'S perception
While CATHERINE'S greed and evil deeds
make her reek with DECEPTION

When DONELY learned I was in town and asked me what I know
I'd look him in the eye and say, "I love LUCY COE!"
Yes a HARDY welcome I will find becomes reality
When I make a guest appearance in PORT CHARLES by the sea

A.M.L.

I never knew that I could love you
More each passing day
And now another year, my love
Has somehow slipped away

You are my tomorrows
And all my dreams come true
You fill my skies with rainbows
As I walk life's path with you

This Way

Hand prints tattle from the wall
Made by someone very small
Pitter patter down the hall
… A child passed this way
Tell-tale cookie crumbs galore
Scattered on the kitchen floor
Made by someone almost four
… A child passed this way
Not allowed beyond the gate
No longer six now turning eight
Now on the street and always late
… A child passed this way
Disrespectful all the time
Takes what's yours – steals what's mine
Done by someone two plus nine
… A child passed this way
Hateful nasty words and then
Sneaks and lies and steals again
Done by someone four plus ten
… A child passed this way
A shackled teen of sixteen years
Brings to life a mom's worst fears
Heartache and a million tears
… My child passed this way

Teas

You took pastel colored flowers
Pretending each was wrapped in lace
And laid one beside each teacup
Marking everybody's place

You gave Teddy yellow
Pretending it was honey
The orange one – a carrot
Crispy fresh for Mrs. Bunny

White for me because you know
I like it when it snows
And purple by your teacup
'Cause that's where purple goes

We talked and laughed while
Evening shadows stole the afternoon
And all too quick it seemed
The party ended much too soon

That day so long ago remains
A treasured memory
When you placed a pastel flower
Beside my cup of tea

Glisten

Outside our home snow soft and white
Brings picture postcard scenes tonight
Inside our home loves afterglow
Warm in your arms I watch it snow

Smile

Just a note to say I love you
And hoping it will find
A smile dance across your face
Each time I'm on your mind

Though out of sight not out of mind
Across the many miles
Just close your eyes and think of me
My heart can feel your smiles

Misses

At day's end when evening comes
My prayer begins like this
Now I lay me down to sleep
Please bless the one I miss

Mister

Thanking you with love, mister
For moments shared with our big sister
And for all the sites and little towns
Filled with memories to jot down
So before our pens run out of ink
We thank you, mister, for the drink

Heeling

Please know I say this from my heart
For you've been on my mind
And these words don't come as easy
As ones hurtful and unkind

I'm sorry, please, forgive me
For I've come to realize
The meaning of sincerity
I apologize

Sky High

I know there's pot in heaven
And let me tell you why
It's filled with marijuana clouds
'Cause angels sing on high

Plus

The sum of me and you is two
The sum of me and you make 'we'
Now add the love we share and see
The 'some' of you and me makes three

My Love

The splendor found within your arms
The magic of your kiss
The happiness you give to me
... Nothing compares to this
You are my world, my better half
My lover and my friend
I know life holds no guarantees
I know all good things must end
So if I awoke tomorrow
And found that you were gone
I'd close my eyes and think of you
For strength to carry on
I'd tuck you deep within my heart
And live my whole life through
Rememb'ring all the love we shared
Forever missing you
But tonight your moonlit silhouette
Beckons me once more
I'm lost within your magic
As we knock on splendor's door
Entwined in passion time stands still
My heart – skips a beat
I only know I love you
With you I am complete

Warmed

May the spirit of Christmas
Glow in your heart
Warmed by fond memories
Though we're apart

For I want you to know
My heart is warmed, too
With the spirit of Christmas
And mem'ries of you

Joy

Warm holiday wishes
Are coming your way
Bringing you joy
For a bright Christmas Day

And hoping the man
In the furry red suit
Will breeze through your house
And leave some of his loot

Fostered Prayer

A miracle sent from heaven
Is how you came to be
God found a heart where you could grow
Is how you came to me

He knew you needed lots of love
To grow up proud and saw
That nowhere else on earth but here
Would you be loved by all

Each time I kneel and say my prayers
I count my blessings, too
For in all the world God's perfect heart
Gave me the gift of you

Flame

Not just a face, nor just a name
My son's friend I call him Flame
His voice is still, his smile – gone
But in my heart he will live on

Now it is time for us to stand
And offer up a helping hand
To end the violence in the 'hood
Turn things around and do some good

How many children must we lose?
Before we walk in other's shoes?
How many tears must we all shed?
How many brothers must lie dead?

For guns don't settle any scores
They only open prison doors
The same is said about a knife
It only gets you five to life

And who are we to stand and judge?
Especially when we hold a grudge
Or when someone don't think our way
We jack 'em up and make 'em pay

So who among us will be first?
To walk away when being cursed
Or say I'm sorry when they're wrong
Or show a child they do belong

The time has come to set things straight
To rid ourselves of wont and hate
To find within ourselves some pride
To walk together side by side
I'm sayin' now it's got to end
Before we lose another friend

S. G. McAfee

Treasures

As sure as precious summer rain quenches all that thirst ... As sure as ocean
Foam crown waves rush in to kiss the earth ... As sure as golden sunrise glides
Across the sunset sky ... As sure as there's a heaven I'll remember you and I
For fate made me your sister long before hearts made us friends
And no one knows where life will lead or just what God intends
But as sure as warm beneath the snow life begins anew
My heart holds treasured mem'ries of a childhood
Filled with you

Still

I lingered in home's doorway
Gazing at the sunset sky
Then turned to face the silence
And my heart began to cry

I closed my eyes as mem'ries rushed
To bring a sense of calm
A dozen years, a million tears
I still miss you, Mom

Purr-rfect Friend

You pounced into my life
Purr-rmiting me to be a part
Of a long and purr-rfect friendship
Leaving paw prints on my heart

You purr-rsevered to teach me
Trust is something that you earn
Love is patience wrapped in kindness
You asked nothing in return

Your purr-rfect place in all the house
Was lying next to me
Oh, how I long for yesterday
The way it used to be

When evening shadows cross the room
And climb my empty chair
I know heaven now is purr-rfect
For my purr-rfect friend lies there

Stray

I knelt to coax the little stray
Shivering in the cold
Inhumane acts had left their scars
Was the story her eyes told

She walked with tail between her legs
A frayed rope trailed there, too
Reminding her of bondage
And the horrors that she knew

I cut the captor from her neck
Its captive made no sound
But cringed and tried to shield her face
As the rope fell to the ground

"Don't hurt me," her eyes pleaded
My eyes begged for her to stay
I gathered her close to my heart
Then stood and walked away

Yo

In crowded cell you sit alone
In prison garb so far from home
And when they say you're finally free
I hope you say, "It's up to me."

Just thought I'd write and drop a line
Hope you're well and feelin' fine
Glad to hear you're doin' good
We're missin' you around the 'hood

All's well here, about the same
Besides there's no use to complain
It's just a test for hangin' in
We smile and bear it with a grin

Frankie's learnin' not to spend
He tries to save some now and then
I'm so proud he's learned a trade
If he keeps it up he'll have it made

Randi's still a would-be mom
Christopher is all but calm
Frank and I just keep it real
We're old enough to know the deal

Hoping they have let you teach
You never know just who you'll reach
To bring a change makes you feel proud
Like turn a mob into a crowd

So live life's puzzle piece by piece
And find that wonders never cease
If you're not sure ask someone, yo
If you don't ask you'll never know

And maybe while you're reading this
Randi Lyn will have her little miss
You're always in my thoughts and prayers
You're not alone … someone cares

MeYou

I'll breathe you in when thunder whispers
I'll hear you move among the leaves
And there in distant evening shadows
I'll hear your call on gentle breeze

I'll find you in a dream at twilight
Your kiss on wings of butterfly
I'll see your path on wintry blanket
Your mem'ry there in summer sky

Now go and take your place in nature
The way that you were meant to do
I'm grateful for our time together
Forever – I'll remember you

Jessa

I smell salt in the air
Feel the wind in my hair
Seagulls call to me
Just out of reach

I find shells in the sand
Oh, there's nothing so grand
As a day with my Nan
Down the beach

Mourning Glory

Warm coffee cups, sleepy eyes and yawns to greet the morning
skies –They start this day in city New – Full schedules planned much
work to do –Twins stand tall with shadows cast – Unaware what comes to
pass – For blue skies fill with smoke and flame Disbelief from whence it
came – My God, as North begins to choke the South fills with new flame
and smoke – As air delivers futile screams to those who watch horrific
scenes of ones who cling or fall or jump – While rescue climbs from
every pump – And helping hands from city blues bring added strength no
time to lose – But Twins succumb with crumbling groans – They swallow
all; they quell the moans – And pulverized beyond belief their asphalt
snows on city streets –The Pentagon has felt the wrath – Our fourth
cuts a destructive path – Across the land from sea to sea – Our country
falls on bended knee – The whole world mourns, our nation weeps
Nightmares haunt the ones who sleep
Make no mistake we will unite
We've only just begun to fight

Biding

Rest in comfort safe, secure
Until I knock on heaven's door
To tell you I am home to stay
Come take my hand and lead the way

Love, Frankie

Dry your tears for just a minute
There is somethin' I must say
Though the grave makes things so final
Mom, I'm not gone I'm just away
I am near – you cannot see me
Feel that sudden gust of wind
See the flicker of a candle
Feel that feeling from within
I am near, you cannot see me
With the rustle of the leaves
Tell your breaking heart to listen
For my whisper through the trees
I am near, you cannot see me smile
In quiet falling snow
Or my tears among the raindrops
'Cause I didn't want to go
And when loneliness surrounds you, Mom
Or my voice you long to hear
Close your eyes and know I love you
Search your heart, I am right here

Unto

Sparkling dew, blue skies and sunlight
Peeking through green laden trees
Now disbelief unspeakable horror
Grief has knocked me to my knees

No way to quell the tears or heartache
My empty arms fill with despair
Lost and alone in silent darkness
Folding my hands I bow in prayer

Forget-Me-Knot

Go softly with my love, my kiss upon your cheek
Feel now resplendent calm, the wondrous peace you seek
Through golden fields where Queen Anne bow to pink Sweet Pea
Blue Cockle wave to clouds from honeysuckle breeze

And there upon The Hill she waits with open arms
You smile climbing to her with weary struggle gone
When tenderly you whisper, "I am home to stay"
She smiles then gently takes your hand to lead the way

Bo

My gentle friend went home today
There were no sweet good-byes
I saw his struggle for each breath
... Devotion in his eyes

Though weary with discomfort
He nudged my hand and whined
His journey now must be alone
He must leave me behind

The doctor stood beside my friend
Through tears all I could see
His waggin' tail ... a final kiss
He slipped away from me

Sons in My Eyes

Life does not pertain to me anymore
It's been so long now I'm not really sure
I remember when life dealt me laughter and smiles
I imagine before I lost my first child

Over half of my life I have lived in a haze
With mechanical movements I crawl through life's maze
While a semblance of normal (society's way)
Hides a burden of sadness day after day

With the same pasted smiles over tear-dried cheeks
The same empty heartache week after week
Then all of a sudden, lo and behold
It's happened again so I've been told

And my farewell kiss yearns for its place with this son
So let it be written ... so let it be done

Gone

Gone from my eyes, your wondrous smile
Gone from my ears ... Your precious voice
They took your life ... They left mine empty
Gone from my arms ... I had no choice

Tears stain my cheeks where once were kisses
Where once was laughter now disbelief
Gone with my heart ... Now deafening silence
While life goes on I drown in grief

Scattered

She sobs …
Mournful sobs to quell her breaking heart
Soulful sobs to soothe her aching arms
For memories swirl within her helpless mind
Again … his contagious smile
Again … his infectious laugh
Scattering … yet again … in deafening silence
Wiping endless tears
… She sobs

Daddy

It seems like only yesterday
A memory bittersweet
You waltzed me through the living room
As I stood upon your feet

Now as you waltz with Mom through heaven, Dad
Know I'm grateful for the chance
To make that treasured keepsake memory
Thank you, for the dance

Savored

Dare I think about my Tink?
For forty years that's all I've done
Recalling hugs, kisses and laughter
Precious memories one by one

I pull them out … they're never dusty
I savor each and every one
Then tuck them back into my heartache
Treasured memories of my son

Poetree

A tree grows its entire life
Towards the heavens strong and tall
Giving shelter, food and precious shade
To God's creatures great and small

Praise

In hour of darkness - You heard our prayers
Praise be to Thee! Oh! Lord we sing
Your love light shines from sea to sea
Praise be to Thee – Our glorious King!

Feathery

A feather from heaven has come into view
Sending a sign just like all pennies do
Hoping to bring you a glimmer of love
By letting you know you're often thought of

Honor Bright

As I proudly raise
The Stars 'n' Stripes
I'm reminded of the cost
I stand in solemn silence
Bow in prayer for loved ones lost
She is this nation's treasured
Symbol – A grand old emblem
Tried 'n' true – I pledge allegiance
To Old Glory – Our country's own: red, white and
blue – Bright spangled stars broad stripes unfurl
Oh! How they wave from sea to sea! Thank you,
Soldiers, the price you pay to keep us free

Faithful

Through the wildflower fields of heaven
To the eternal pearly gates
Now free from pain and suffering
He lies patiently and waits

Newborn Prayer

My newborn prayer to God above
Please wrap them in your precious love
Please give them strength, the will to live
They have much joy and love to give

S.C.'s Prayer

Thank you for a safe place to play
A warm place to lay
Her kindness and love
Others only dream of

Goes My Heart

A new and exciting time in life
Begins for you today
You chose the path less traveled
A quick kiss then on your way

Now do not limit expectations
Dare to tempt the hands of fate
Success is just around the corner
… Your destiny awaits

Bits 'n' Pieces

Sorrow floods my very being
Life as I know it disappears
My broken heart in bits 'n' pieces
Scatters on a sea of tears

I pray for strength and consolation
I gather pieces as I cry
Your friend ship gathers winds of splendor
Oh! Glorious sails against blue sky

Some bits 'n' pieces drift on ebb tide
They join your wake as you depart
You sail away, dear friend, to glory
With bits 'n' pieces of my heart

A Tear

That's not a tear it's just a memory
Falling softly on my cheek
Just an overflowing thought of you
Unexpected bittersweet

One by one there'll come a hundred more
This is how it always starts
When my soul is filled my eyes can't help but spill
Mem'ries from my broken heart

Randi Lyn

You are my song ... that echoes through the trees down mountainside and floats on autumn breeze with butterfly ... Down past the thicket, winding stream to wildflower fields ... My song so pure and sweet the praying mantis kneels ...Down where the dragonflies dance in first twilight ... And rainbow fades when smiling sun sets out of sight ... Where scent of honeysuckle swirls with fireflies as hummingbirds, bees, frogs and crickets harmonize ...The murmur soon ignites a glorious rhapsody among God's creatures great and small down to the sea ... Where foam-crown waves in rhythm break upon the shore ...Great eagles lift the thundering chorus as they soar ... Then lobo howls her soulful lullaby of love ... She serenades the sleepy moon in clouds above While stars keep time each softly twinkling through the night 'til smiling sun begins anew with morning light ... When echoes through the trees sweet songbirds sing along ...The hills and valleys fill with you ...You are my song

I Said a Prayer

You closed your eyes ... I said a prayer
You slipped away ... Life's so unfair
I miss your smile, your voice, your touch
Forever loved ... God knows how much

Although I know your pain has ceased
For in God's grace you are at peace
There's not a day that passes by
I feel your loss deep down inside

I call your name but you're not there
The sound of silence ... everywhere
My skies of blue have turned to gray
Oh! How I long for yesterday

Emptiness fills this heart of mine
How can that be? Life's so unkind
With thoughts of you my tears begin
Until you fill my arms again

Tomorrows

"Suffer unto me," His soothing voice called from above
Jesus smiled with open arms enfolding you in glorious love
Where found deserved peace and comfort
Where found resplendent wondrous calm
I'll miss you all of my tomorrows
With all my heart I love you, Mom

Too Often

Sometimes it's hard to understand the emptiness inside
Sometimes it's hard to comprehend the world when loved ones die—A prayer to God
For endless tears and sorrow to depart – For cradled in your love they rest in peace tucked in your heart

About The Author

I am the second of four children, born to William and Jane McAfee in Chester, Pennsylvania. As long as I can remember I was fascinated with the rhyming word in songs and nursery rhymes. I loved them. I could listen for hours – which I did. I can still hear my mom singing or reciting Pony Boy, Old MacDonald, Little Man You've Had a Busy Day, Teddy Bear Picnic, Hey Diddle-Diddle, Playmate, Said My Pajamas, Little Miss Muffet, Fuzzy Wuzzy. Before I understood what reading and writing was all about, I began kindergarten at Lincoln School. I could write my name in cursive thanks to my older sister who was in second grade. I would sit alongside of her at the dining room table with pencil and paper drawing her homework. Well, I didn't realize it was homework. I just copied what she did. My sister resented it until my mom explained to her that it was okay for her sister to copy her answers. I drew her spelling, her arithmetic, her name – all of it. I had not a clue what it all meant. I just copied doing my best to make my paper look like hers. Then in first grade Mrs. Cloud taught me the alphabet. In second grade Mrs. Dick taught me spelling and in third grade Miss Harley taught me cursive. It all came together. Letters make words, words make stories. And I could put my words on paper to make my own stories. They had given me their secret! They had opened the world to me. I loved my elementary teachers – all of them.

I remember walking past Dad in the living room sitting behind his newspaper. I slowed my gait and peered at the back of his paper. There were tiny words all over the pages. Tiny words I could read! Words could be any size! (I was really impressed with billboards). Dad laid the paper on his lap showing me the comics. I read them out loud giggling at Popeye, Nancy and Sluggo, Blondie, Sad Sack, Lulu and Pricilla's Pop who, by the way, ate mashed potato sandwiches. I still do.

When I was nine or ten, I remember Mom and Dad purchasing a set of World Book Encyclopedias which came with a set of Child Craft Books. One of the books was nothing but nursery rhymes. Imagine! All the rhymes my Mom had taught me! And then some! On more than one occasion, as memory serves me, I sat in our tiny kitchen at the table to read out loud from this book and giggled repeating a rhyme I had learned at her knee. She would stir or mix or boil or thicken while joining me in verse.

I began writing my own rhyming words at the age of eleven. As my life unfolded, I graduated from high school and the Institute of Children's Literature correspondence course. I waited on Bingo players at fourteen, babysat, was a Fuller Brush Girl, a cook, a jewelry associate, cashier and a barmaid. I lubricated ball bearings, sold motorcycle parts and worked in the wiring department at Vertol where we slipped notes, phone numbers and women's measurements into the thirty-two feet long electrical harnesses we prepared to be used in the fields of Vietnam. My poetry draws its breath from personal experience – innocence, love, faith, tragedy, happiness, loss of two of my three children. God gave me a gift … I share it with you.

www.ingramcontent.com/pod-product-compliance
Lightning Source LLC
Chambersburg PA
CBHW060337130626
46553CB00003B/1038